The Question & Answer Book

ALL ABOUT SOUND

ALL ABOUT SOUND

By David Knight
Illustrated by Lewis Johnson

Troll Associates

Library of Congress Cataloging in Publication Data

Knight, David C.
　　All about sound.

　　(The Question and answer book)
　　Summary: Questions and answers provide basic informa-
tion about sound, including its formation, pitch,
variety, mode of travel, echo, and how ears receive sound
waves.
　　　1. Sound—Juvenile literature. [1. Sound.
2. Questions and answers]　I. Johnson, Lewis, ill.
II. Title.　III. Series.
QC225.5.K54　1983　　　534　　　82-17387
ISBN 0-89375-878-7
ISBN 0-89375-879-5 (pbk.)

Printed in the United States of America
10　9　8　7　6　5　4　3　2　1

What do you hear?

Close your eyes for a minute and listen. Listen to the sounds around you. They are probably the sounds you hear every day. You may hear a clock ticking…voices…or the honk of a car's horn.

On other days you might hear the patter of rain and the rumble of thunder. You might hear a bird singing and the wind blowing in the trees. These are common sounds—yet each one is different from all the others.

How many sounds do you hear?

Try to think of the sounds you hear every day. If you could write them all down, you would have a very, very long list.

How are all sounds alike?

You could probably name thousands of sounds, and each one would be a little different from all the rest. But all sounds *are* alike in one way. They are made by something that is moving.

Strike a bell. Then touch it. You'll feel the metal moving. Strum a guitar. Then feel the strings. They are moving.

When you speak, something inside your throat moves. Put your finger on your throat. Then hum a long note. You will feel the vocal cords inside your throat moving. Remember, for a sound to be made—any sound—something has to be moving.

The kind of movement that makes sound is "back and forth" movement. Scientists call this movement *vibration*. Stretch a rubber band tightly between your thumb and second finger. Now twang it. The sound you hear is the rubber vibrating back and forth.

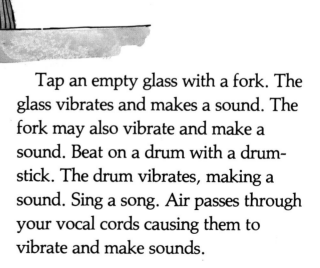

Tap an empty glass with a fork. The glass vibrates and makes a sound. The fork may also vibrate and make a sound. Beat on a drum with a drumstick. The drum vibrates, making a sound. Sing a song. Air passes through your vocal cords causing them to vibrate and make sounds.

Try this experiment.

As soon as something stops vibrating, the sound stops. You can prove this with a simple experiment. Tie a piece of string around the handle of a fork. Hold the other end of the string, and hit the fork with something, to make the fork vibrate. You will hear the sound from the vibrating fork. Then stop the vibration by grasping the end of the fork. As soon as the vibration stops, the sound stops.

How do we recognize different sounds?

One way is by listening to how high or low a sound is.

Try singing the lowest note you can. Then sing the highest note you can. Scientists say that the low note has low *pitch*. The high note has high pitch. Pitch is the lowness or highness of a sound. When your vocal cords change from one note to another, the sound of your voice changes its pitch.

But what makes the pitch of a sound high or low?

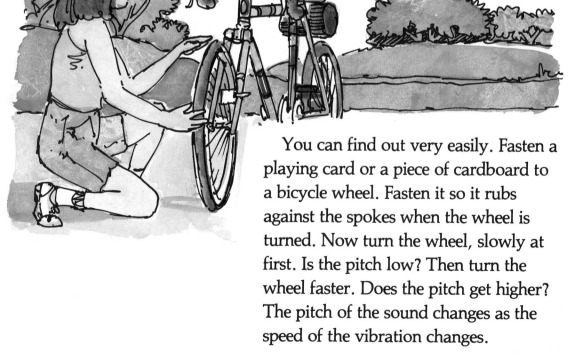

You can find out very easily. Fasten a playing card or a piece of cardboard to a bicycle wheel. Fasten it so it rubs against the spokes when the wheel is turned. Now turn the wheel, slowly at first. Is the pitch low? Then turn the wheel faster. Does the pitch get higher? The pitch of the sound changes as the speed of the vibration changes.

When something vibrates slowly, the pitch of the sound is low. When it vibrates more quickly, the pitch becomes higher. You have probably heard the low, deep noise a foghorn makes, and the shrill, high pitch of a police officer's whistle. Which sound is made by faster vibrations?

Some sounds are very, very high. They are so high that people cannot even hear them. Sounds like these are called *ultrasonic* sounds. Some animals, like dolphins, can make such sounds. Dogs can hear the sound of special high-pitched whistles that people cannot hear.

How do sounds travel?

Every day, we hear thousands of sounds—people talking, music playing, telephones ringing. But how do these sound vibrations reach our ears?

Sounds need something to travel *in* or *through*. They need something to carry them along. Scientists have a name for anything that carries sound. They call it a *medium*.

The most common medium that carries sound is air. Air is made of oxygen, nitrogen, and other gases, all mixed together. But sound can travel through many other things, too. Water, glass, and iron are just a few of the things that can carry sound.

Try an experiment. Find a long iron fence, and put your ear against one end of it. Then have a friend go to the other end of the fence. Have your friend tap the fence with a stick. You will hear the sound vibrations as they travel through the iron.

Here is another experiment.

This one will show you *how* sound moves. Drop a pebble into a quiet pool of water. Do you see the ripples? They're like tiny waves, spreading out through the water in all directions.

As sounds travel, they behave very much like these tiny water waves. But they are called *sound waves*.

Air is made up of tiny bits of matter called *molecules.*
Molecules are too small to see, even with a powerful
microscope. But scientists know molecules are in the air,
and how they behave.

What happens to the molecules in the air when you
twang a rubber band? First, the rubber band vibrates
outward. It pushes against the nearby air molecules. The
molecules push against *other* air molecules. And *those*
molecules push against still *other* molecules.

Then, when the rubber band moves in the other
direction, the air molecules try to move back.

But the rubber band vibrates outward again, and starts pushing against the air molecules again. These moving molecules make sound waves in the air. Like the ripples in a quiet pool, sound waves travel outward in all directions.

We could not hear any sounds at all if there were no medium for sound vibrations to travel through. On the moon, there is no air. There is nothing to carry sound waves along. So when astronauts walked on the moon, they could not hear one another speak the way they could on Earth. Instead, they spoke to each other by radio. This is because radio waves are different from sound waves. They don't need any medium to travel through.

Did you ever watch a baseball game from high up in the bleachers?

If you did, you may have noticed something strange. When the batter hit the ball, you didn't hear the sound until a moment later.

Or did you ever look out a window during a thunderstorm? If you did, you may have seen a huge flash of lightning sizzle across the sky. But you may not have heard the thunder caused by the lightning until a few seconds later.

Sound vibrations take *time* to get from one place to another. Scientists have found out that sound vibrations travel more quickly in certain kinds of matter than in others.

It takes about one second for sound vibrations to travel 1,087 feet (331 meters) through the air. But those same sound vibrations will travel more than four times faster through water. Sound moves fastest through certain solid things, like metal. Sound travels fifteen times faster through steel than it does through air!

SOUND MOVES THROUGH AIR AT 1,087 FEET PER SECOND.

SOUND IN WATER IS 4 TIMES FASTER THAN IN AIR!

SOUND MOVES THROUGH STEEL... 15 TIMES FASTER THAN THROUGH AIR!

Why do sound waves travel more quickly through water and some solid things than they do through air?

Because the molecules in water and certain solid things are more *elastic* than air molecules. This means that they are very flexible—or easily bent and shaped. For example, think of how metal wire can be twisted and shaped. It also can be twisted *back* into the shape it was before. The molecules of metal wire are said to be very elastic. Molecules that are elastic can bump against each other quickly. They pass sound waves along faster and better than air does.

You can prove that sound travels through some solids better than it does through air. First, make a simple tin-can telephone. Get two empty coffee cans and connect them with a very long piece of wire. Then hold one can, and give the other to a friend. Stretch the wire tightly between the cans. Whisper something to your friend over the "phone." Then whisper something *without* using the "phone." Which carried the sound vibrations of your voice better—the air or the solid metal wire?

Sometimes sound waves do strange things.

Have you ever shouted out across a valley or canyon?
If you have, you may have heard a ghostly voice
repeating your words. Of course, the ghostly voice is
really your own. What you hear is an *echo*.

What is an echo?

Echoes are sound waves that bounce back to your ears. If you stand about 55 steps away from a brick wall on an empty playground and shout, the sound waves of your voice bounce off the wall and return to you. You hear them as an echo. But why do they bounce back?

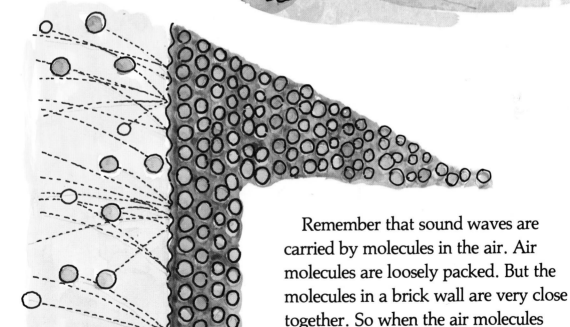

Remember that sound waves are carried by molecules in the air. Air molecules are loosely packed. But the molecules in a brick wall are very close together. So when the air molecules strike the wall, they bounce off. And the sound waves they carry are sent back as an echo.

Sailors make good use of echoes. They use echo-sounding machines to bounce sound waves off the ocean floor. Then they wait for the sound waves to return to their ships. The amount of time this takes tells them how deep the water is.

Bats use echoes to fly safely about in the dark. They send out high-pitched sounds that bounce off trees, rocks, or other things they might fly into. The return echoes warn the bats if danger is near.

Sometimes echoing sound waves can be a nuisance. In large auditoriums and theaters, too many sound waves may bounce around all at once. This makes it very hard to hear what a speaker or actor is saying.

Specially trained people, called sound engineers, are often paid to study such buildings. They try to get rid of the echoes. They may put up special tiles and curtains. These special materials absorb, or soak up, the annoying sound waves.

Sound waves help us to know and understand things around us. Each time we speak and listen, a message is being sent and received. Sounds also warn us of danger, they give us music, and they help us in many other ways.

But all the sound waves in the world would be of no use if you could not *hear* them.

28

How do your ears hear sound waves?

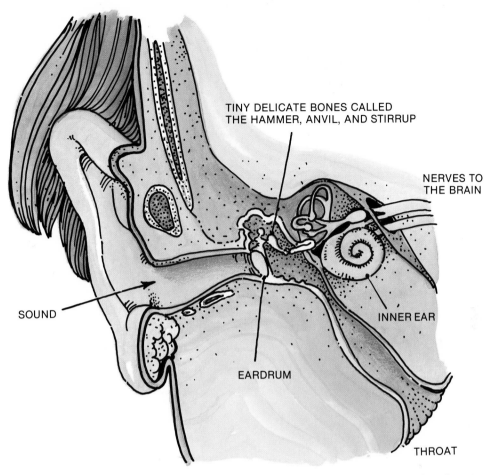

TINY DELICATE BONES CALLED
THE HAMMER, ANVIL, AND STIRRUP

NERVES TO
THE BRAIN

SOUND

INNER EAR

EARDRUM

THROAT

When sound waves enter your ear, they reach your eardrum. The eardrum is well named. It is very much like a tiny drum inside your ear. The thin membrane of the eardrum vibrates the way a drum does when it is played. Your vibrating eardrum then passes the sounds along to tiny, delicate bones farther inside your ear. These bones pass the vibrations along to your inner ear. Finally, your nerves carry the message of the vibrations to your brain.

That message may be the sound of ocean waves crashing at the seashore. Or it may be the high-pitched sound of sea gulls as they soar overhead. Or it may be the sound of children, shouting and playing on the sandy beach.

That message may be the sound of a power lawn mower roaring along. Or the buzz of a mosquito outside your window on a warm summer evening. Or the plop of the newspaper, as the paper carrier tosses it on your porch.

The message that reaches your brain could be almost anything, because the world is filled with all kinds of sounds. And each sound you hear is different from every other sound. Each has its own special vibrations and pitch.

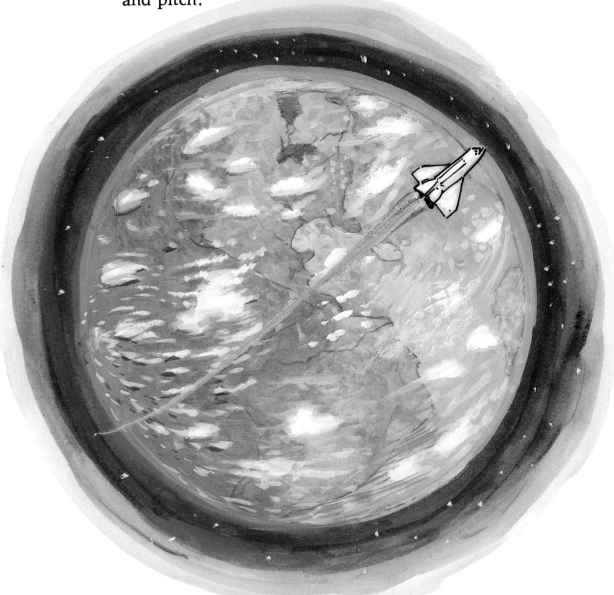

What do you hear right now?

Close your eyes...and listen!